HR-approved Ways to Tell Coworkers They're Stupid

PRUDENT PRES

The Email Avalanche.

"Did you get my email?"

"Yes, I'm just sifting through my inbox now."

"Found it!
Buried under the
digital landslide."

The Mysterious Printer

Can you fix the printer?
It's acting up again."

"I'll give it a look."

"Time to negotiate with the
temperamental ink beast."

The Coffee Conundrum

"Who finished the coffee and didn't make more?"

"Not sure, but I'll start a new pot."

"Ah, the daily 'who-dunnit' brew mystery."

The Monday Blues

"How was your weekend?"

"Too short, as always!"

"A fleeting glimpse of freedom, now back to the grind."

The Unending Conference Call

"Isn't this call productive?"

"Definitely covering a lot of ground."

"If by 'productive' you mean perfecting my doodling skills."

The Password Puzzle

"Forgot your password again?"

"Just resetting it for security reasons."

"Yes, for the 47th time this month."

The Meeting That Could've Been an Email

"Wasn't that meeting crucial?"

"Certainly informative."

"A masterclass in wasting everyone's time."

The Lunch Thief

"Did you see who took my lunch from the fridge?"

"No idea, that's unfortunate."

"The office fridge saga continues..."

The Dress Code Debacle

"Do you like the new dress code?"

"It's an interesting choice."

"Perfect if we're auditioning for 'Corporate Drab: The Musical'."

The Holiday Party Planning

"Excited for the office holiday party?"

"It's always a unique experience."

"As exciting as watching paint dry – but with eggnog."

The Phantom Urgency

"Can you drop everything? This is urgent!"

"Right on it!"

"Adding it to the pile of 'urgent' things from last week."

The Spreadsheet Sorrows

"Who loves working with spreadsheets?"

"They certainly are useful."

"Ah yes, digital torture sheets."

The Wifi Woes

"Is the WiFi down for you too?"

"Seems like it."

"The perfect excuse to stare at a blank screen."

The Perpetual Latecomer

"Running late again?"

"Yeah, traffic was a nightmare."

"By 'traffic', I mean my bed held me hostage."

The Eternal Optimist

"Isn't this a great place to work?"

"It has its moments."

"If by great you mean soul-sucking."

The Copycat Colleague

"Did you notice Tom is copying your style?"

"Imitation is the sincerest form of flattery."

"Great, I have a style stalker."

The Office Gossip

"Did you hear the latest office rumor?"

"I try to stay out of it."

"Time for the daily soap opera update."

The Excessive Delegator

"Can you handle this task for me?"

"I'll see what I can do."

"Oh, found my name in the 'dump tasks here' box again."

The Unforgettable Presentation

"How was my presentation?"

"Very memorable."

"Memorable like a root canal."

The IT Illusionist

"Why is the computer always crashing?"

"Might be some technical glitch."

"Because it's possessed by the spirit of obsolescence."

The "Voluntary" Overtime

"Can you stay late tonight? We need all hands on deck."

"I'll see what I can do."

"Sure, I had no plans other than living my actual life."

The Feedback
Fiasco

"Can I give you some feedback?"

"Of course, always happy to improve."

"Brace for impact, here comes the 'constructive criticism' cannonball."

The TMI Colleague

"Did I tell you about my latest diet?"

"I think you mentioned it, yes."

"Only about a million times. Spoiler: I still don't care."

The Walking Dead(line)

"Why does everything become urgent at the last minute?"

"Just the nature of the business, I guess."

"Because planning is a foreign concept here."

The Break Room Baffler

"Who keeps leaving dirty dishes in the sink?"

"Not sure, but we should all try to clean up after ourselves."

"Probably the same phantom who 'forgets' their smelly leftovers."

The Mystery of the Missing Stapler

"Have you seen my stapler?"

_____

"No, haven't seen it."

_____

"Check the black market of office supplies, along with my vanished sanity."

The Conference Call Carousel

"Why don't you turn your video on during calls?"

"Oh, just bandwidth issues."

"So you can't see my soul leaving my body."

The Houdini Holiday

"Are you taking a vacation this year?"

"Haven't planned it yet."

"Planning an escape? More like a daydream at my desk."

The Inspirational Quote Inquisition

"What do you think of the motivational posters around the office?"

"They're interesting."

"Nothing screams 'inspiration' like a cat hanging from a branch."

The Perpetual Promise

"When will they fix the air conditioning?"

"They said soon."

"Right after hell freezes over, apparently."

The Diet Destroyer

"Who brought donuts again?"

"Not sure, but it's a nice gesture."

"The office's secret plan to ruin diets and widen waistlines."

The Truth About Teamwork

"Isn't teamwork our greatest strength?"

"Absolutely, we do better together."

"If by 'teamwork' you mean 'group procrastination sessions.'"

The Silent Sufferer

"Why don't you ever complain?"

"Just trying to stay positive."

"Because screaming internally is my superpower."

The Meeting Marathon

"Ready for another 3-hour meeting?"

"Let's get it done."

"Only if it's followed by a 3-hour nap."

The Phantom Pay Raise

"Heard anything about pay raises?"

"Not yet, but I'm hopeful."

"I've seen unicorns more often than our pay raises."

The Bathroom Breakdown

"Why is the bathroom always occupied?"

"Popular place, I guess."

"The last refuge for the overworked and underpaid."

The Elevator Eulogy

"Awkward silence in the elevator, huh?"

"It's just a quiet morning."

"It's where small talk and joy come to die."

The Car Park Catastrophe

"Why is parking here such a nightmare?"

"It's always busy."

"Because it's designed by someone who clearly hates cars... and people."

The Exit Interview Irony

"Will you miss this place after you leave?"

"It's been an experience."

"Miss it? I'll be too busy celebrating my parole from this corporate jail."

The Never-Ending Story

"Why does this project keep dragging on?"

"Just lots of details to iron out."

"Because it's a cursed relic from the productivity graveyard."

The Casual Friday Farce

"You excited about casual Friday?"

"It's a nice change."

"Oh, absolutely. Can't wait to downgrade my misery to 'business casual.'"

The Annual Review Antics

"Think you'll get a good review this year?"

"I sure hope so."

"As good as anyone can under a microscope and a magnifying glass."

The Health Hazard

"Why is the office kitchen always a mess?"

"People must be busy."

"Because cleanliness is too much to ask from grown adults apparently."

The Technological Time Travel

"Why is our software so outdated?"

"Budget constraints, maybe?"

"Because our IT budget is apparently a time capsule from 1995."

The Promotion Illusion

"Think you'll get that promotion?"

"I'm optimistic."

"Sure, right after pigs enroll in aviation school."

The Water Cooler Wasteland

"Heard any good gossip lately?"

"I try to stay out of it."

"Only the usual circus of who's backstabbing who this week."

The Potluck Peril

"You going to the office potluck?"

"I might stop by."

"Only if I fancy a round of Russian Roulette with mystery casseroles."

The Holiday Party Hypocrisy

"Looking forward to the office holiday party?"

"It should be interesting."

"Can't wait to see hypocrisy and forced merriment on full display."

The Out of Office Odyssey

"How come you're never at your desk?"

"Just a lot of meetings."

"Because that's the only way to escape the soul-sucking vortex."

The Brainstorm Blunder

"What do you think of our brainstorm sessions?"

"They're... interesting."

"A perfect storm of aimless chatter masquerading as ideas."

The Suggestion Box Satire

"Ever put anything in the suggestion box?"

"A couple of times."

"Yeah, a note that said, 'Try using this for recycling.'"

The Phantom Flexibility

"Isn't our work schedule flexible?"

"It has its moments."

"As flexible as a concrete slab."

The Lunch Hour Lament

"Why is the cafeteria food so bad?"

"It's not for everyone."

"Because taste is a luxury we clearly can't afford."

The Corporate Jargon Jumble

"What's with all the corporate jargon in meetings?"

"It's just industry speak."

"A desperate ploy to make empty ideas sound profound."

The Disappearing Desk Dilemma

"Why is your desk always so clean?"

"I like to keep things organized."

"So I can make a quick getaway when the time comes."

The Birthday Bash Boredom

"Excited for the office birthday party?"

"It's always nice."

"As exciting as watching paint dry... if the paint was also singing off-key."

The Wellness Program Parody

"What do you think of the new wellness program?"

"It's an interesting initiative."

"Ah, the corporate version of putting a Band-Aid on a bullet wound."

The Exit Strategy

"Any plans after quitting this job?"

"Exploring a few options."

"Celebrating my release from this corporate penitentiary."

The Office Plant Plight

"Why do all the office plants die?"

"Maybe they need more care."

"Probably losing the will to live, like the rest of us here."

The Glacial IT Response

"Why does IT take ages to respond?"

"They must be really busy."

"Or they're in a time warp where one day equals a year."

The Mirage of Meritocracy

"Do you believe promotions are merit-based here?"

"I'd like to think so."

"And I'd like to think calories don't count on weekends."

The Recycling Bin Rendezvous

"Who keeps leaving stuff beside the recycling bin?"

"Maybe they're just forgetful."

"Or training for the 'Laziest Person Alive' championship."

The Incompetent Incognito

"How does he always escape work unnoticed?"

"He's probably just really efficient."

"Yeah, at being a professional ghost."

The Conference Room Chronicles

"Isn't it hard to find an available conference room?"

"Can be challenging at times."

"Like finding a unicorn in a haystack."

The Art of Unread Emails

"Why don't people read their emails properly?"

"Maybe they're overwhelmed."

"Or practicing for the 'Ignorance is Bliss' Olympics."

The Printer Poltergeist

"Why is the printer always jammed?"

"Just bad luck, I guess."

"Or it's possessed by a demon that feeds on frustration."

The Casual Day Charade

"Do you enjoy casual Fridays?"

"It's a nice break from the norm."

"As if jeans magically make this place less soul-crushing."

The Meeting Room Mirage

"Ever notice meeting rooms are always booked but empty?"

"Maybe plans change."

"Or they're mirages, illusions of productivity."

The Vacation Vanishing Act

"How do you feel coming back from vacation?"

"Refreshed and ready to go."

"Like I've just returned from Narnia and reality is a slap in the face."

The Great Escape Fantasy

"Ever daydream about quitting dramatically?"

"I think we all have our moments."

"All the time, complete with a smoke bomb and theme music."

The Flawed Fire Drill

"Why are fire drills always so disorganized?"

"It's hard to coordinate everyone."

"Because rehearsing chaos is our true company policy."

The Fridge Funk Odyssey

"What's with the smell in the office fridge?"

"Someone must've forgotten their lunch."

"Or it's a new biohazard experiment."

The Cubicle Confessions

"Do you like working in a cubicle?"

"It's cozy enough."

"It's like a hamster cage, minus the wheel and joy."

The Happy Hour Hypocrisy

"Enjoying the team happy hour?"

"It's nice to bond outside work."

"It's like being at work, but with alcohol and forced smiles."

The Mute Button Mystery

"Why do people forget to mute on calls?"

"Just an oversight, I guess."

"Because sharing their personal life's soundtrack is their gift to us all."

The Peculiar Promotion Protocol

"How does he get promoted despite doing nothing?"

"Maybe he's got hidden talents."

"Or photos of the boss at last year's Christmas party."

The Battle of the Thermostat

"Why's the office temperature always extreme?"

"Hard to please everyone."

"It's a weather simulation: Sahara desert meets Arctic tundra."

The Ghost of Projects Past

"Remember that project we never finished?"

"Vaguely, it was a while ago."

"It haunts me at night, whispering 'what if.'"

The Sarcasm Blindspot

"Do people get your sarcasm at work?"

"Sometimes they do."

"Only when I wrap it in a neon sign flashing 'JOKE'."

The Perennial Password Reset

"Why do I always have to reset my password?"

"It's for security reasons."

"It's like a never-ending game of 'Guess What I'm Thinking' with the computer."

Made in the USA
Monee, IL
05 December 2023

48286200R00046